A First Word Bank

Ruth Thomson

Chrysalis Education

US publication copyright paperback © 2006 Chrysalis Education
US publication copyright hardcover © 2004 Chrysalis Education
Published in conjunction with Chrysalis Books Group Plc

Distributed in the United States by
Smart Apple Media
2140 Howard Drive West
North Mankato, Minnesota 56003

Text © Ruth Thomson 2002
Illustrations © Chrysalis Books Group Plc 2002

ISBN 1-931983-09-7 (hc)
ISBN 1-59389-246-2 (pb)

Library of Congress Control Number 2002 141338

Editor: Mary-Jane Wilkins
Designers: Rachel Hamdi, Holly Mann
Illustrators: Patrice Aggs, Becky Blake, Louise Comfort, Charlotte Hard, Brenda Haw, Jan McAfferty, Kevin McAleenan, Kevin Maddison, Holly Mann, Melanie Mansfield, Colin Payne, Lisa Smith, Sara Walker, Gwyneth Williamson
Educational consultant: Pie Corbett, Poet and Consultant to the National Literacy Strategy
Printed in China

Contents

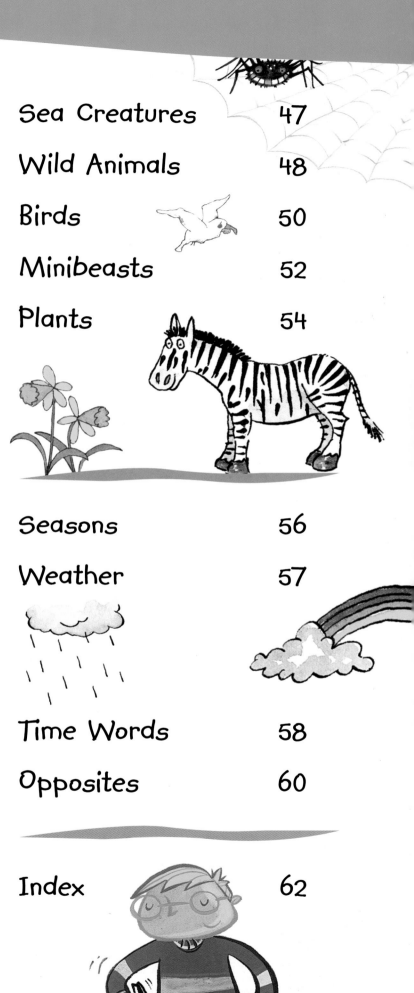

About this Book

This word bank is a resource of carefully chosen words to help young children develop their vocabulary.

How to use this book

Every spread can be used for discussion, for playing word games, to provide words for writing, and as a spell-check.

The illustrated words are divided into categories. Some are labeled as examples for children to follow. A useful word box lists adjectives, verbs, or extra nouns.

Children can also think up their own words and sentences. Try brainstorming ideas on a theme before children start to write.

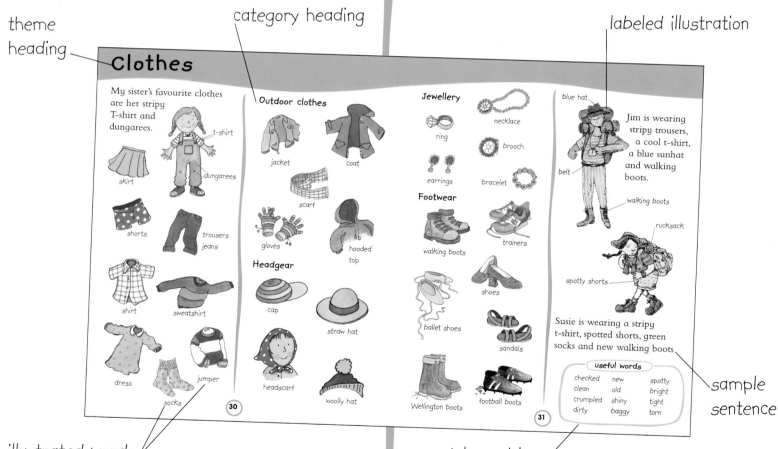

The words are arranged by theme and also by type of writing. Each spread gives a choice of words on a theme and a sentence that shows some of the words in use.

Types of writing

Writing has many different purposes, language features, and forms. The types of writing that children initially learn are laid out in the chart on the right.

Text type	Purpose	Features	Word bank themes
Labels	✧ Identification	✧ Often written as single words ✧ Usually nouns ✧ Sometimes used with lines or arrows connected to the the picture	✧ Parts of a bicycle (16) ✧ Parts of a spaceship (17) ✧ School Equipment (18–19) ✧ Machines (27) ✧ Parts of the body (28) ✧ Parts of a cat (44) ✧ Parts of a bird (50) ✧ Parts of an insect (52) ✧ Parts of a plant (54)
Lists	✧ Reminders ✧ Planning	✧ Written in note form ✧ Each item written on a separate line	✧ Going Shopping (40–41)
Reports Doctors look after people who are hurt or ill. Some work in hospitals. They treat people and give them medicines to help make them better.	✧ To describe things or people: their qualities, behavior, habits, or uses	✧ Written in the present tense, eg Trees are plants. ✧ Non-chronological ✧ Focuses on the general rather than an individual, e.g. Doctors take care of sick people. Not Dr. Parks takes care of Sam.	✧ My Home (22–23) ✧ Buildings (24–25) ✧ Tools and Machines (26–27) ✧ Describing People (28–29) ✧ Clothes (30–31) ✧ People at Work (32–33) ✧ Meals (42–43) ✧ Animals (44–53) ✧ Plants (54–55) ✧ Seasons/Weather (56–57)
Recounts At the weekend Dad took us to a theme park. First we swung on the swingboats. Then we rode on the roller coaster. After that we queued for a turn on the big wheel.	✧ To retell events	✧ Written in the past tense, eg I went to the park. ✧ In chronological order, ie first, next, after, last. ✧ Focus on a particular person or people, e.g. I, he, she, we, they, Jim.	✧ My News (8–9) ✧ Party Time (10–11) ✧ In the Park (12–13) ✧ Vacation Time (14–15) ✧ A Day at School (20–21) ✧ My Home (22–23) ✧ Time Words (58–59)
Explanation	✧ To explain how things work or why something happens	✧ Written in the present tense, eg You push the pedals of a bike.	✧ Ways to Travel (16)
Stories One day she met a friendly dragon.	✧ To entertain	✧ Written in the first or third person (I, he, she) and usually written in the past tense ✧ Chronological ✧ About human or animal characters—good and bad ✧ May include dialogue ✧ Use adjectives and powerful verbs	✧ Story Characters (34–35) ✧ Story Creatures (36–37) ✧ Story Objects (38–39) Useful words also appear in: ✧ My dream factory (27) ✧ Describing People (28–29) ✧ Clothes (30–31) ✧ Weather (57) ✧ Time Words (58–59)

Word Games

You can use the themed spreads to play all sorts of word games. These will help children expand their vocabulary, develop their reading skills, and improve their memory and concentration.

I went to market

Play this old favorite with the Shopping spread *(pp. 40–41)*. The first player says:

> I went to market and bought some apples.

The next player repeats the sentence, adding a new item:

> I went to market and bought some apples and some cheese...

Change the game by asking players to add an adjective to their word, such as its color or shape. Players can also choose a food item in alphabetical order, e.g., apples, bananas, carrots, etc.

Vary the game by changing the place or situation, e.g.

> I went on vacation and took...*(p. 14)*

> I went to a restaurant and ordered...*(p. 42)*

> I went to the toy store and bought...*(p. 11)*

> I opened the treasure chest and found... *(p. 38)*

What is it?

Take turns describing three features of a wild animal using the pictures *(pp. 48–49)* to help you, e.g.

> This animal is brown, shaggy, and has horns.

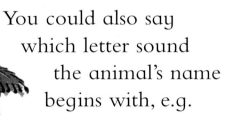

You could also say which letter sound the animal's name begins with, e.g.

> This hairy animal begins with y *(yak)*.

You could add extra information, e.g.

> This black-and-white animal is very smelly.

Dressing up

Take turns dressing up a person, using the clothes pictures *(pp. 30–31)*. Each player chooses a person and a garment, plus an adjective that begins with the same letter, saying, e.g.

I will dress a boy
in shiny shorts.
or
I will dress a fine lady
in a crooked crown.
or
I will dress a girl
in old overalls.

They can go on to invent some other outfits, e.g.

a gorgeous gown or clumping clogs

What's my job?

One player chooses one of the people at work *(pp. 32–33)*, but doesn't tell the other players which one it is. The other players ask questions in turn to find out which person it is, e.g.

Do you work outside?	Yes
Do you help build houses?	No
Do you keep the streets clean?	Yes
Are you a street cleaner?	Yes

You could also play this game with story characters *(p. 34)*.

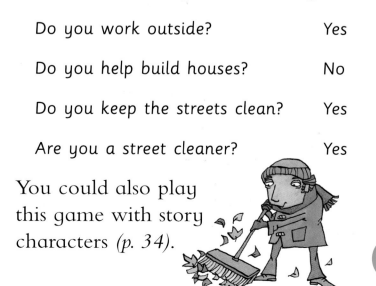

Making sentences

Open the book at any theme. Take turns choosing two words on that theme and ask the other players to make up as many sentences as they can using both words, e.g. mouse, bone:

The mouse found a bone.

The mouse hid behind a bone.

A bone is bigger than a mouse.

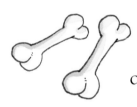 When no one can think of any more, choose another pair of words.

Mystery objects

Take turns thinking of an object. Say what it is, e.g.

It is a vegetable.

Describe what it looks like, e.g.

It is long, hard, and orange.

Say where it is found (or what it is used for), e.g.

It grows underground.

It can be eaten raw or cooked.

Can other players guess what it is? Use pictures of home *(pp. 22–23)*, tools *(p. 26)*, clothes *(p. 30)*, and story objects *(p. 38)*.

My News

Places

On Saturday afternoon Mom and Dad took us to the movies. After that, I stayed over at Sam's house and we played with his kitten. On Sunday we went for a bike ride.

movies
film

park

country

outdoor market

friend's house

Grandma's house

restaurant

museum

show

theme park

carnival

Activities

rode my bike

watched TV
watched a video

Keep out!

made a den

played a board game

flew my kite

practiced the recorder

washed the dog

played with the dog

went rowing

played baseball

went shopping

did a jigsaw puzzle

drew some pictures

useful words

sister	cousin	visited
brother	uncle	saw
grandma	aunt	watched
friend	grandpa	drove

Party Time

rabbit   astronaut   cat   pirate   King   flower   cowboy

Costume party

On Saturday, I went to
Jamie's costume party.
Joe dressed up as a pirate
and I went as a cat.
A clown did funny tricks,
and we played hide-and-seek.

fairy

princess and prince

pop stars

Party things

candy

streamers

magician entertainer

balloons

invitation

birthday cake

birthday cards

clown

Presents

bike

ball

camera

gloves

yo-yo

car

scarf

goggles

crayons

game

bracelet

globe

CD

piggy bank

kite

glider

fish tank

skates

sketchbook

robot

book

kitten

recorder

jeep

teddy bear

stuffed animal

jigsaw puzzle

fort

In the Park

Yesterday we met some friends in the park for a game of frisbee.

frisbee

grass

birds

boat

fountain

swing

soccer ball

slide

path

gardener

scooter

bridge

jungle gym

sandbox

ducks

tree

flower bed

picnic

useful words

played	climbed	found
kicked	ran	walked
fed	watched	slid
threw	hid	rode

Last weekend Dad took us to an amusement park. First we swung on the swing boats. Then we rode on the roller coaster. Last, we waited in line to ride the Ferris wheel.

Ferris wheel

roller coaster

carousel

water slide

bumper cars

simulator

fun house

swing boats

octopus ride

entrance

line

helter-skelter slide

candy

crowd

lollipop

cotton candy

13

useful words

crashed	twisted	glided
smashed	plunged	whirred
splashed	rolled	rocked
spun	whirled	zoomed

Vacation Time

Places to go

For our summer vacation, we went to the seashore. We played on the beach every day.

seashore

town
city

mountains

river

country

Things to take on vacation

backpack

sunscreen

T-shirt

camera

suitcase

swimsuit

flashlight

skis

sandals

flippers

map

bat

ball

towel

goggles

blanket

tent

frisbee

At the seashore

gull

One day we built an enormous sandcastle and decorated it with stones and shells. After that we buried Dad in the sand.

sandcastle

shells

pail

cliffs

surfer

surfboard

rocks

crab

fishing boat

waves

ocean

In the country

butterfly

farm

bees

tractor

field

hive

birds

rooster

flowers

sheep

fence

hill

forest
woods

useful words

dug	climbed	explored
waded	collected	made
swam	walked	pretended
threw	watched	met

Ways to Travel

Parts of a bicycle

brake

seat

handlebars

reflector

pump

fender

tire

back wheel

chain

pedal

spokes

You push the pedals of a bike to make the wheels turn. The faster you pedal, the faster the bike goes.

On land

tricycle

racing car

motorcycle

truck

car

van

train

bus

tractor

useful words		
key	seat belt	steering wheel
start	brake	gearshift
stop	gas	windshield
engine	helmet	accelerator

On water

rowboat

tugboat

trawler
fishing boat

sail boat

ocean liner
ship

speedboat

In the air

airplane
jet

helicopter

glider

hot-air balloon

In space

To take off into space you climb up the ramp into the rocket. You strap yourself in and press the buttons to start the countdown. Then you blast off.

rocket

Parts of a spaceship

porthole

ladder

doorway

fin

exhaust

feet

ramp

useful words

zoom	skim	liftoff
land	sail	soar
speed	flash	roar
whir	hurtle	whiz

School Equipment

We made labels for everything in our classroom.

globe

puppets

blocks

clock

pencil sharpeners

scissors

rulers

crayons

pencils

pens

string

glue

coat hooks

trays

shelves

books

chairs

pillows

stuffed toy

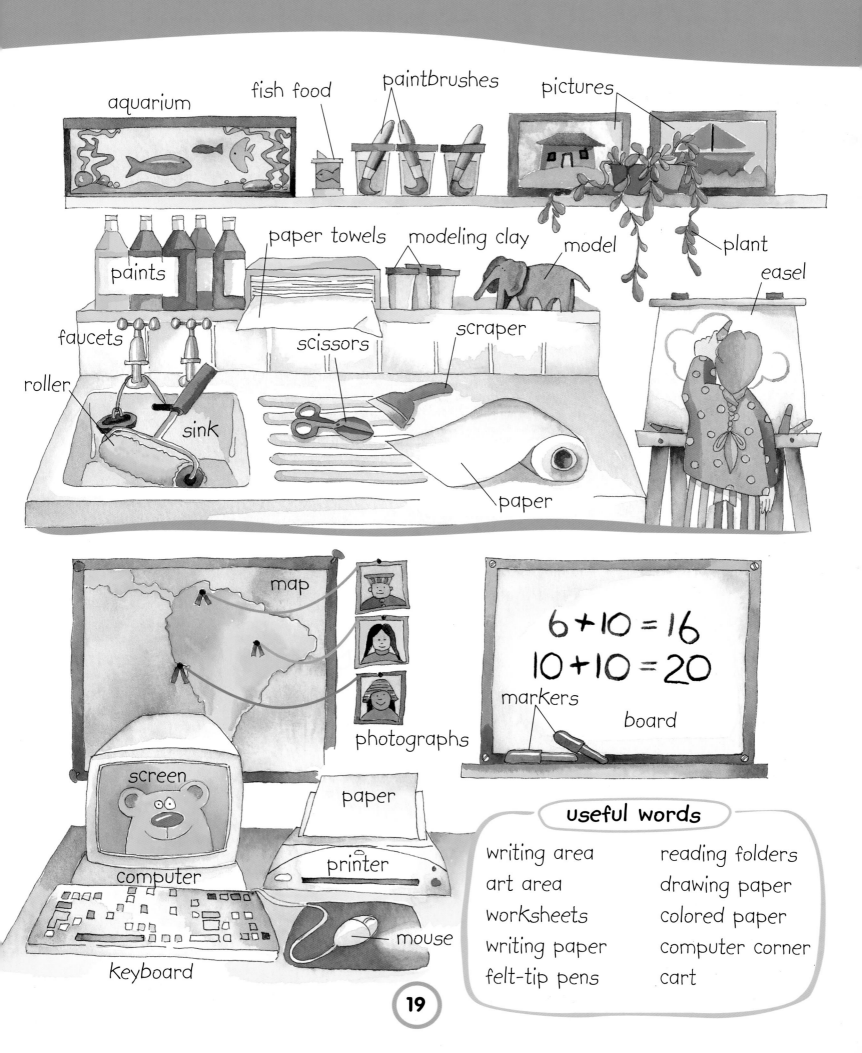

aquarium

fish food

paintbrushes

pictures

paints

paper towels

modeling clay

model

plant

easel

faucets

scraper

roller

scissors

sink

paper

map

$$6 + 10 = 16$$
$$10 + 10 = 20$$

markers

board

photographs

screen

paper

computer

printer

keyboard

mouse

useful words

writing area	reading folders
art area	drawing paper
worksheets	colored paper
writing paper	computer corner
felt-tip pens	cart

A Day at School

Today we are making paper butterflies. We are cutting them out of shiny paper.

counting

reading

measuring

weighing

sorting

writing

dancing

comparing

imagining

planting

painting

gluing

making

drawing

looking at

coloring

playing

Yesterday we talked about insects.

sang

pretended

clapped

watched

useful words

compared	cut	read
painted	counted	made
measured	wrote	drew
looked at	played	glued

My Home

Where do you live?

I live in an apartment on the third floor.

house

apartment house

Living room

sofa

mirror

fish tank

armchair

vase

lamp

telephone

television

What is your bedroom like?

I share a bedroom with my brother. We have bunk beds and loads of toys.

bunk beds

toy basket

radio
boom box

blanket

pillow

Bathroom

soap

sponge

toothpaste

toothbrush

soap dish

faucets

towel

bathtub

Kitchen

clock

refrigerator
fridge

stool

table

high chair

tray

broom

Dinnerware

dishes

teapot

saucers

cups

sugar bowl

bowl

dinner
plates

salad
plates

platter

gravy boat

Utensils

grater

whisk

Knife

cutting board

dish towel

wooden spoon

saucepan

frying pan

pitcher

fork

strainer

colander

scale

mixing bowl

Buildings

offices

houses

hotel

bank

movie theater

department store

market

city hall

garage

pet shop

café

school

At the garage you can buy gas. You can watch films at the movie theater. At the outdoor market you can buy fruit and vegetables.

24

useful words

work	learn	make things
worship	stay	get married
eat	drink	get better
get money	swim	play ball

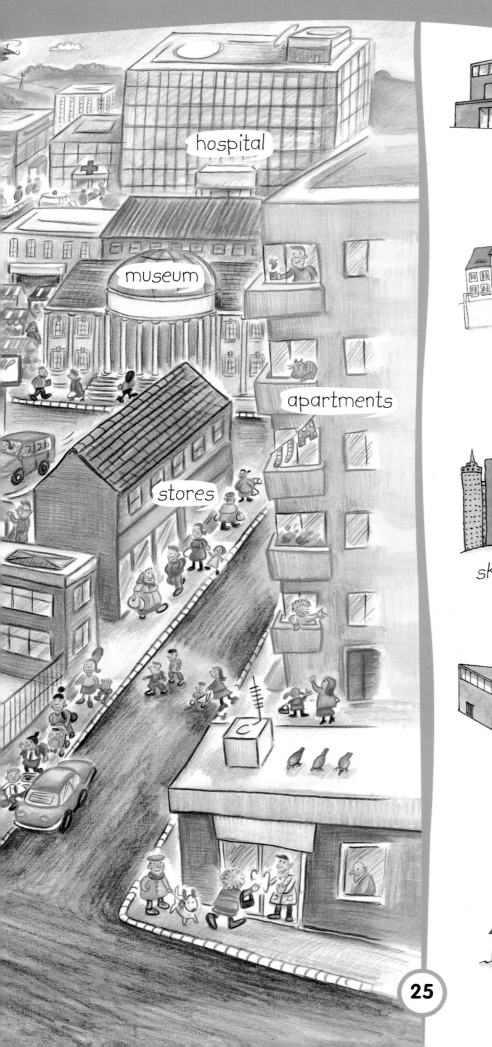

hospital

museum

apartments

stores

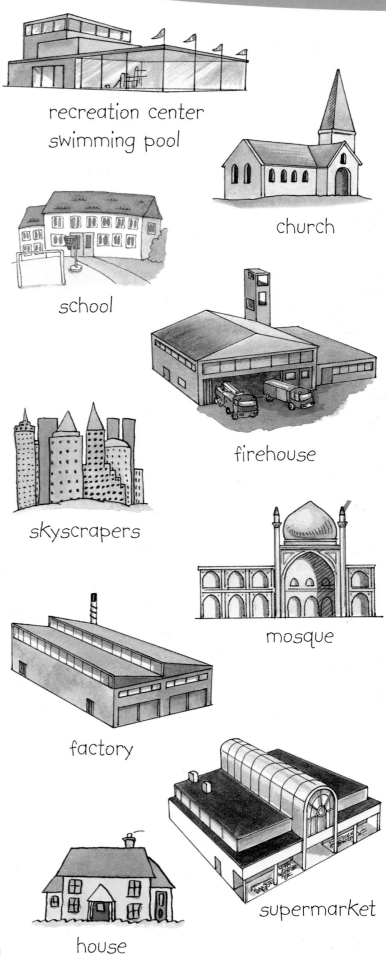

recreation center
swimming pool

church

school

skyscrapers

firehouse

mosque

factory

supermarket

house

Tools and Machines

Building tools

A saw has a metal blade with sharp teeth. It is used to cut wood.

screw

saw

pliers

toolbox

hammer

screwdriver

mallet

wrenches

nail

drill

Painting tools

paintbrush

paint

roller

ladder

Gardening tools

rake

spade

hose

fork

ax

wheelbarrow

lawn mower

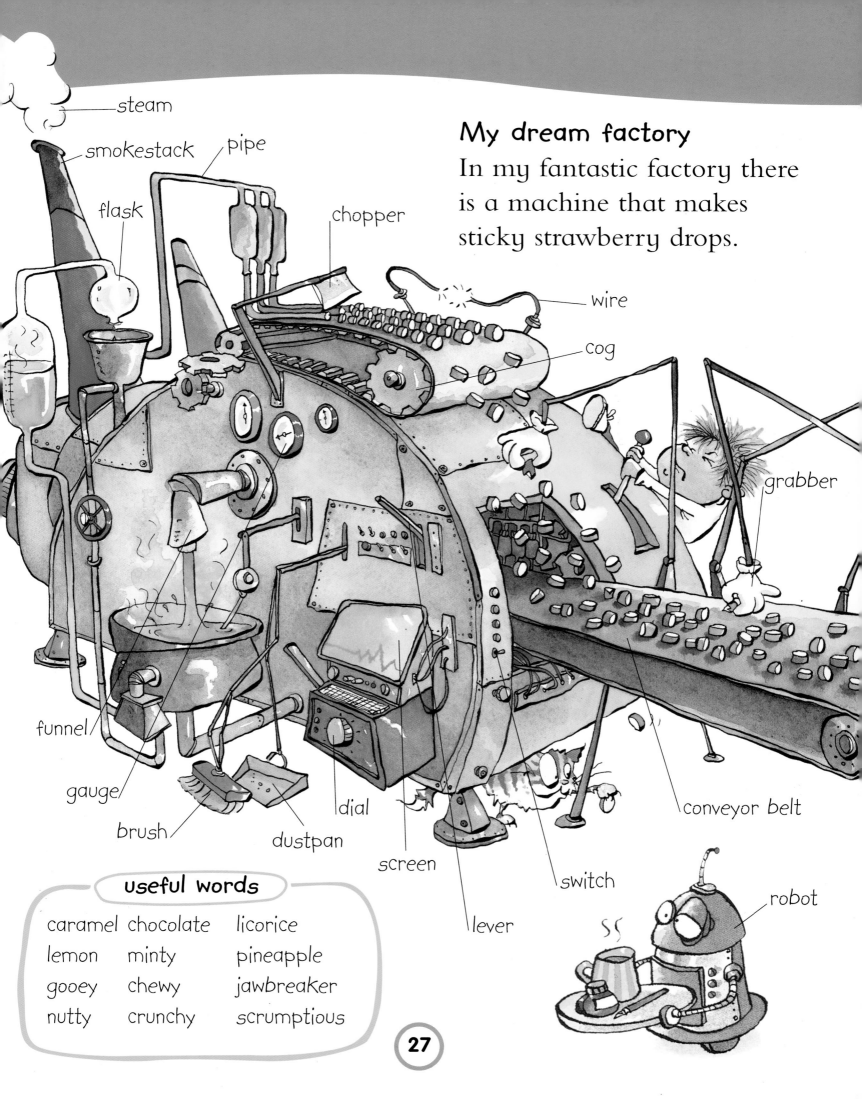

steam

smokestack

pipe

flask

chopper

My dream factory
In my fantastic factory there is a machine that makes sticky strawberry drops.

wire

cog

grabber

funnel

gauge

brush

dustpan

dial

screen

conveyor belt

switch

lever

robot

useful words

caramel	chocolate	licorice
lemon	minty	pineapple
gooey	chewy	jawbreaker
nutty	crunchy	scrumptious

27

Describing People

Parts of the body

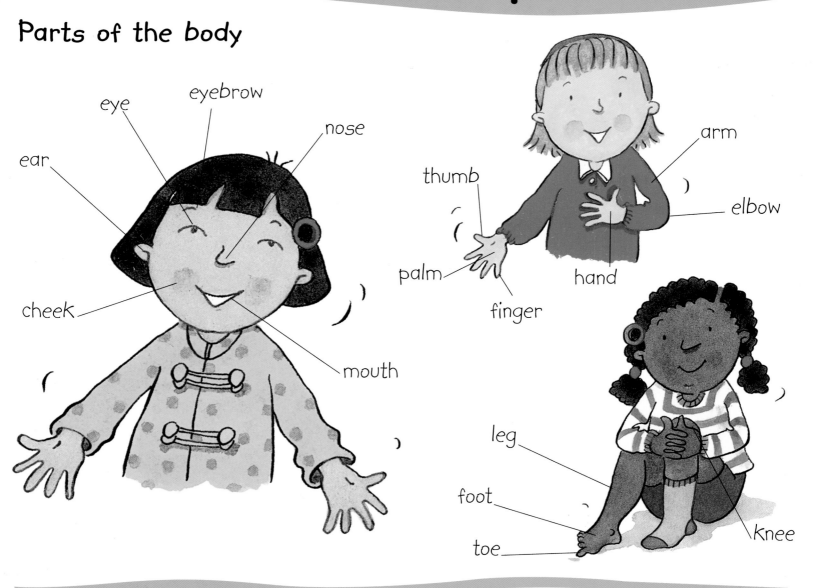

eye
eyebrow
nose
ear
cheek
mouth
thumb
arm
elbow
palm
hand
finger
leg
foot
knee
toe

Hair

curly
long
pigtails
short
dark
fair

What people look like

old

fat
plump
stout

young

strong
muscly

thin
skinny

long nose

dark hair

pale skin

knobby knees

thin legs

narrow feet

Jane is tall and has dark hair.

red hat

round nose

short legs

small feet

Ben is short and has
a round nose.

Clothes

My sister's favorite clothes are her striped T-shirt and overalls.

T-shirt

overalls

skirt

shorts

pants
jeans

shirt

sweatshirt

dress

socks

sweater

Outdoor clothes

jacket

coat

scarf

gloves

hooded top

Headgear

cap

straw hat

headscarf

ski cap

Jewelry

ring

necklace

pin

earrings

bracelet

Footwear

hiking boots

sneakers

ballet shoes

shoes

sandals

rubber boots

soccer cleats

blue sunhat

belt

striped pants

hiking boots

Jim is wearing striped pants, a cool T-shirt, a blue sunhat, and hiking boots.

striped T-shirt

polka-dot shorts

new boots

Susie is wearing a striped T-shirt, polka-dot shorts, green socks, and new hiking boots.

useful words

check	warm	trendy
clean	old	bright
crumpled	shiny	tight
creased	baggy	torn

People at Work

builder

garbage collector

bus driver

pilot

bricklayer

plumber

truck driver

mechanic

window cleaner

street cleaner

racing driver

messenger

writer

photographer

TV cameraperson

computer operator

teacher

10 + 4 =
20 + 4 =
30 + 4 =

newsanchor

32

supermarket worker

waiter

ballet dancer

storekeeper

baseball player

soccer player

gardener

vet

farmer

hairdresser

dentist

optometrist

nurse

doctor

Doctors take care of people
who are hurt or sick.
Some work in hospitals.
They treat people
and give them medicines
to help make them better.

33

Story Characters

Once upon a time, there was a lonely princess.

People

witch

thief

queen

prince

princess

sailor

shepherd

soldier

family

king

pirate

old man and old woman

farmer

giant

mermaid

Goldilocks

emperor

elf

clown

Knight

She lived all alone in a palace tower.

palace

fort

cottage

tower

castle

village

useful words

beautiful	sad	rich
charming	poor	silly
cruel	powerful	wicked
happy	pretty	young

Story Creatures

One day she met a friendly dragon.

dragon

bear

lion

cat

hen

monkey

mouse

dinosaur

alien

gingerbread man

troll

crocodile

toad

goats

36

fox

frog

fairy

monster

pig

horse

genie

wolf

He took her for a walk in the dark forest.

forest

swamp

lake

mountains

cave

desert

useful words

crafty	hairy	timid
enormous	huge	tiny
fierce	proud	ugly
gentle	silent	wise

37

Story Objects

The dragon showed the princess a magic treasure chest.

treasure chest

sword

rope

invitation

goblet

veil

basket

mirror

crown

present

fire

ring

key

glass slipper

wand

coins

throne

mask

book of spells

turban

witch's hat

When the princess opened the lid, smoke billowed out, hiding everything from view...

well

telescope

smoke

flying carpet

fountain

coach and horses

spaceship

feast

boat

clock

ship

moon

island

army cavalcade

Going Shopping

I helped Mom write our shopping list. Then we went to the market to buy all the food.

Groceries

jam

rice

eggs

cheese

yogurt

milk

chocolate

butter

ketchup

cookies

bread

spaghetti

Shopping list
Two cartons of milk
A dozen eggs
A loaf of bread
A package of cookies
A pound of butter
Six containers of yogurt
A bunch of bananas

Meat and fish

burgers

ham

fish sticks

fish

chicken

sausages

Vegetables

broccoli

lettuce

peas

cabbage

carrots

mushrooms

cauliflower

sweet potato

cucumber

garlic

onions

pumpkin

beans

potatoes

Fruit

grapes

pineapple

plums

lemons

oranges

tomatoes

apricots

bananas

strawberries

apples

cherries

useful words

jar	bunch	bottle
box	container	bag
package	bar	basket
can	slab	pound

Meals

I have a bowl
of cereal, a glass
of orange juice, and
some toast for breakfast.

jam

orange juice

toast

cereal

bread

hot chocolate

Snacks

cake

muffin

sandwich

cookies

nuts

chips

apple

fruit

cake

My favorite food is chocolate cake. I like it because it is sweet and sticky.

fish

apple pie

chocolate cake

salad

pancakes

baked potato

burger and fries

stew

pizza

soup

fries

spaghetti

chicken leg

omelet

fruit salad

bread and cheese

ice cream

43

useful words

creamy	crunchy	smooth
chewy	gooey	spicy
crisp	juicy	hot
crumbly	mushy	tangy

Pets

My pet

dog

spider

puppies

snake

hamster

mouse

rabbit

parrot

goldfish

cat and kitten

Parts of a cat

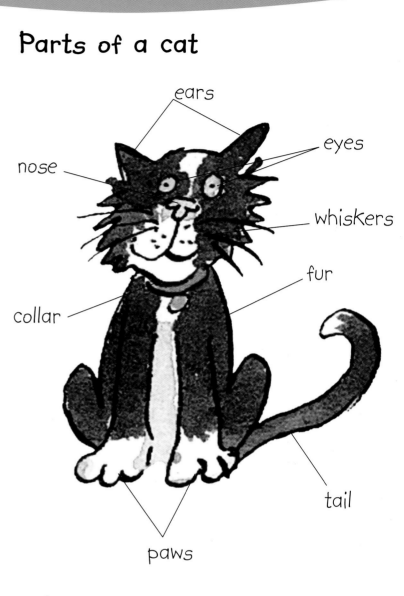

ears

eyes

nose

whiskers

fur

collar

tail

paws

I have a pet cat.
His name is Tom.
He has a soft black coat.
He is bouncy and friendly.

useful words		
noisy	hairy	nosy
clean	dirty	playful
smart	scaly	furry
cuddly	quiet	lazy

Where pets sleep

Tom sleeps on my bed.

armchair

birdcage

fish tank

basket

hutch

jar

What pets eat

Tom eats pet food.

cheese

pet food

lettuce

birdseed

bones

fish

What pets do

When I pet him,
Tom purrs.

run

hide

sleep

play

splash

scratch

useful words

barks	howls	squeaks
growls	screeches	yaps
hisses	snarls	yelps
meows	snuffles	yowls

45

Farm Animals

Chickens lay eggs. They sit on the eggs to keep them warm. Chicks hatch from the eggs. Chicks are baby chickens.

chicks

chicken

rooster

horse   foal

bees
beehive

goat   kid

bull

cow   calf

goose

turkey

donkey

pig   piglet

duck   duckling

sheep   lamb

useful words

sty	stable	gosling
field	barn	larva
pen	pond	scratch
nest	chicken coop	peck

Sea Creatures

Dolphins swim around in families. They talk to each other with clicking and squeaking noises.

dolphins

turtle

whale

starfish

angelfish

shark

seahorse

seal

crab

oysters

lobster

electric eel

jellyfish

coral

useful words

fins	tail	claws
scales	rocks	seabed
glide	cling	dive
float	grow	hide

Wild Animals

An elephant is **enormous**.
It has a long trunk
and sharp tusks.

elephant

monkey

anteater

tortoise

leopard

cheetah

camel

sloth

zebra

orangutan

yak

bear and cub

platypus

reindeer

baboon

kangaroo

lizard

crocodile

koala

skunk

beaver

tiger

panda

lion

giraffe

hare

snake

otter

antelope

deer

fox

wolf

useful words

furry	humongous	rough
tiny	playful	speedy
fierce	sleek	strong
smelly	hairy	huge

Birds

Parts of a bird

beak

eye

feathers

wing

claws

talons

tail

Owls are birds of prey.
They have large round eyes.
They sleep during the day
and fly at night.

eagle

hawk

vulture

parrot

goose

ostrich

swallow

seagull

swan

stork

flamingo

peacock

Where birds live

Owls live in farm buildings, hollow trees, or caves.

towns

cliffs

fields

mountains

caves

woods
trees

marsh

river

Owls lay eggs. They make a nest for the eggs. The eggs hatch into chicks.

Bird food

Owls hunt at night for small animals, such as mice.

mice

berries

ants

grubs

worms

frog

nuts

seeds

fish

insects

useful words		
build	hover	perch
catch	roost	search
flap	dive	soar
glide	peck	swoop

Minibeasts

Parts of an insect

All insects have a head, a thorax, an abdomen, and six legs. Some have wings.

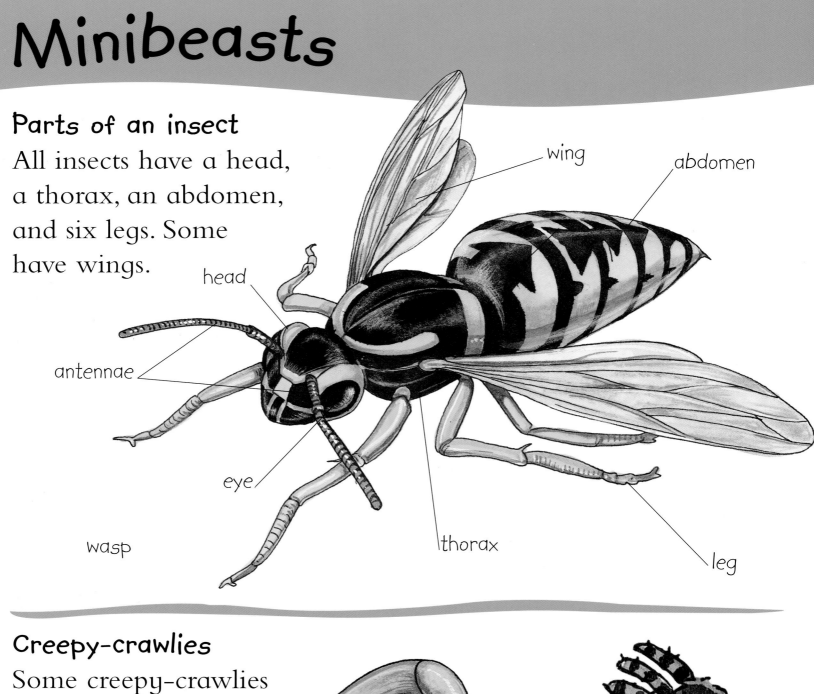

wing

abdomen

head

antennae

eye

wasp

thorax

leg

Creepy-crawlies

Some creepy-crawlies have lots of legs. Slugs and snails have no legs at all.

slug

spider

snail

worm

woodlouse

centipede

Insects

mosquitoes

fly

beetles

butterfly

caterpillar

dragonfly

grasshopper

ants

bee

glowworm

ladybug

Where minibeasts live

Some insects live on plants and eat leaves. Spiders spin sticky webs to catch insects.

web

plant

nettles

pond

flowers

tree

grass

wall

useful words

burrow	grow	lay
crawl	curl	scuttle
dart	hide	shelter
flutter	jump	wriggle

53

Plants

Plants begin as seeds. They need water to help them grow. They also need plenty of sunshine.

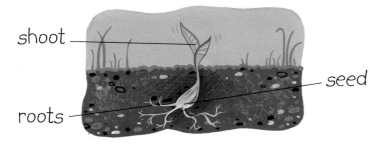

shoot

roots

seed

Parts of a plant

flower

seeds

petals

leaf

A sunflower can grow to be taller than a person. In the summer it has a big yellow flower. The flower turns to face the sun.

stalk

veins

Flowers

bluebell

daffodils

waterlily

tulip

rose

sunflower

crocuses

wild roses

useful words

spring	warm	buds
summer	cold	petals
fall	rain	stamens
winter	soil	sepals

Parts of a tree

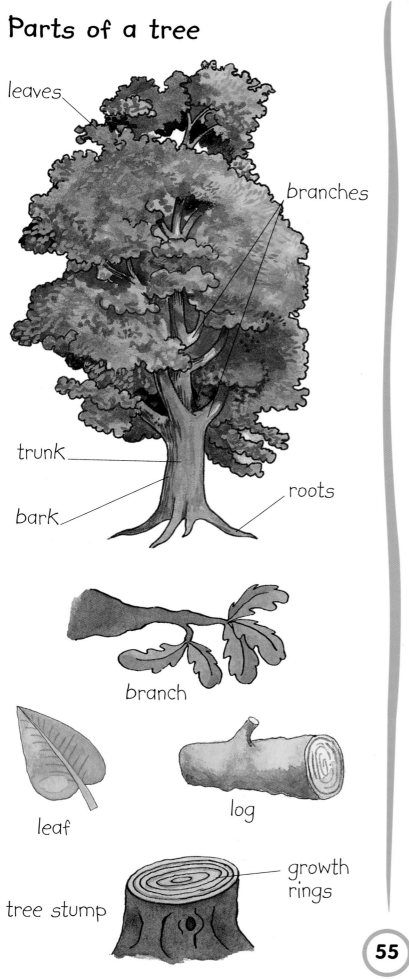

leaves

branches

trunk

roots

bark

branch

leaf

log

tree stump

growth rings

Trees

Oak trees lose their leaves every fall. Pine trees keep their leaves all year round.

oak

palm tree

beech

pine

yew

Tree fruits

pine cone

holly berries

acorn

horse chestnut

Seasons

In the spring, new leaves grow and blossom appears.

In the fall, the leaves turn red and gold and fall off the trees.

Weather

The sky turned dark. Lightning snaked through the sky. Thunder crashed like cymbals. Fat raindrops splashed on our heads.

rainy

windy

cold

snowy

storm

storm cloud

lightning

cloud

sun

puddle

rainbow

rain shower

icicles
frost

raindrops

warm
hot

mist
fog

useful words

poured	cool	bitter
shone	mild	dripped
blazed	dry	spattered
froze	chilly	as bright as

Time Words

Days of the week

Monday

Tuesday

Wednesday

Thursday

Friday

Saturday

Sunday

On Monday we flew to the country. Then we drove to a campsite and set up our tent. On Tuesday morning we searched for buried treasure.

Months of the year

January	July
February	August
March	September
April	October
May	November
June	December

calendar

My birthday is on May 20th.

Times of day

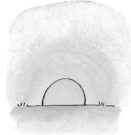

dawn
daybreak

morning

noon

afternoon

dusk
sunset

night

moon

stars

midnight

Telling the time

01:00	one o'clock
02:00	two o'clock
03:00	three o'clock
04:00	four o'clock
05:00	five o'clock
06:00	six o'clock
07:00	seven o'clock
08:00	eight o'clock
09:00	nine o'clock
10:00	ten o'clock
11:00	eleven o'clock
12:00	twelve o'clock

useful words

first	yesterday	after
next	today	eventually
then	tomorrow	last
later	before	finally

Opposites

cold

hot

Winter weather can be cold and snowy.

In the summer the weather can be hot and sunny.

fast

slow

short

tall

happy

sad

young

old

clean

dirty

up

down

shout

whisper

catch

throw

old

new

CINEMA

empty

full

open

shut

small

big

above

top

below

bottom

timid

brave

high

low

asleep

awake

messy

neat

61

Index